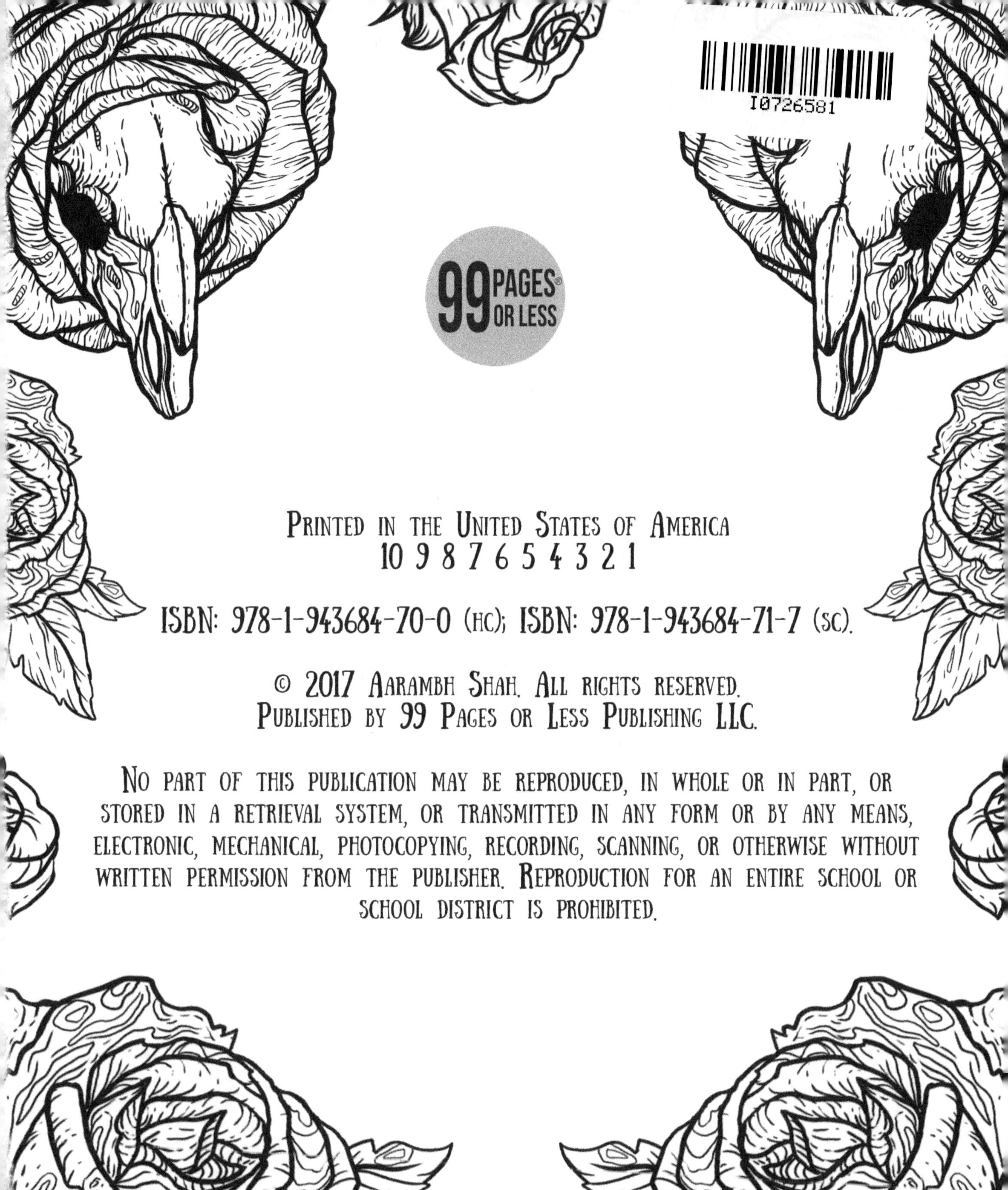

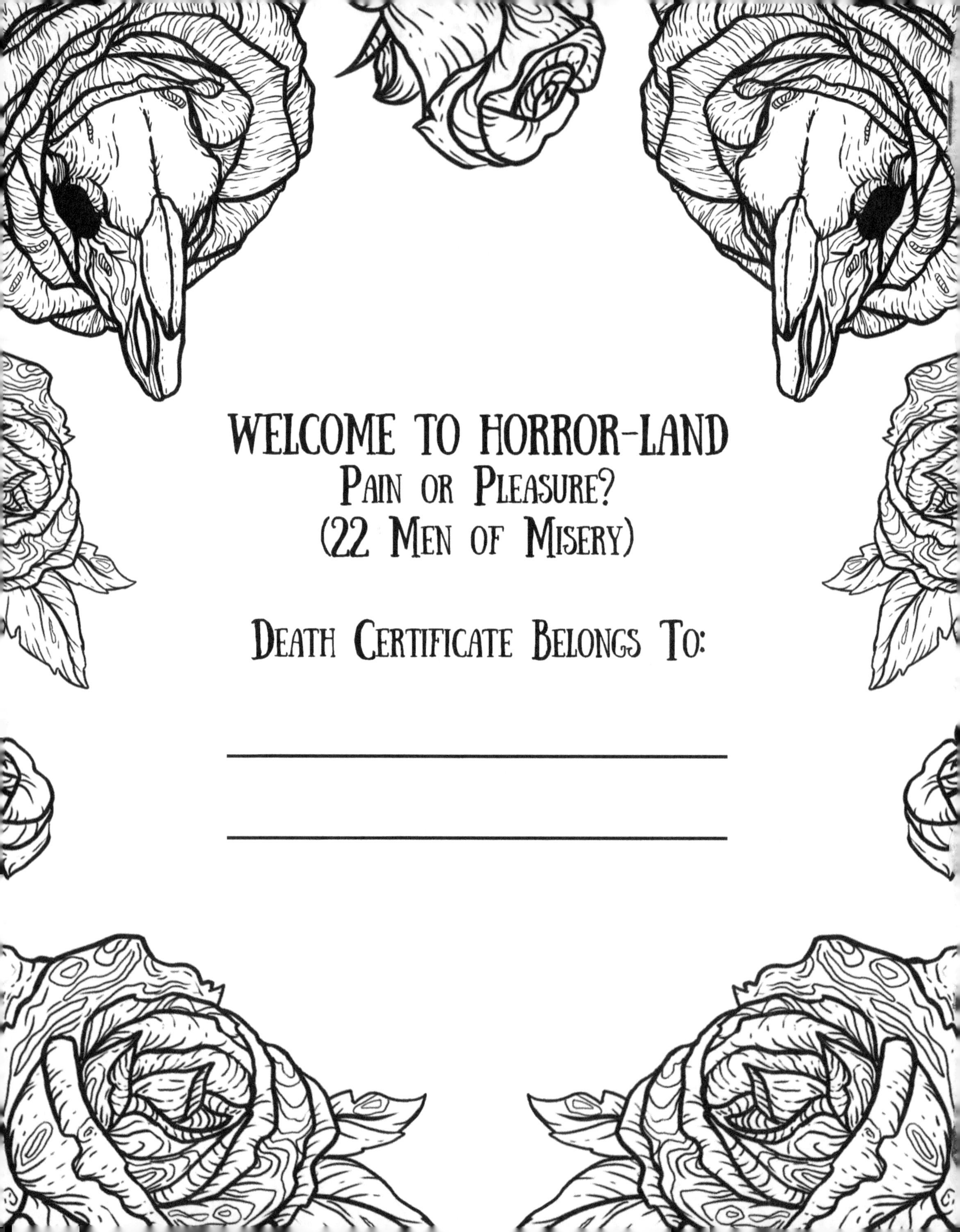

WELCOME TO HORROR-LAND
Pain or Pleasure?
(22 Men of Misery)

Death Certificate Belongs To:

____

____

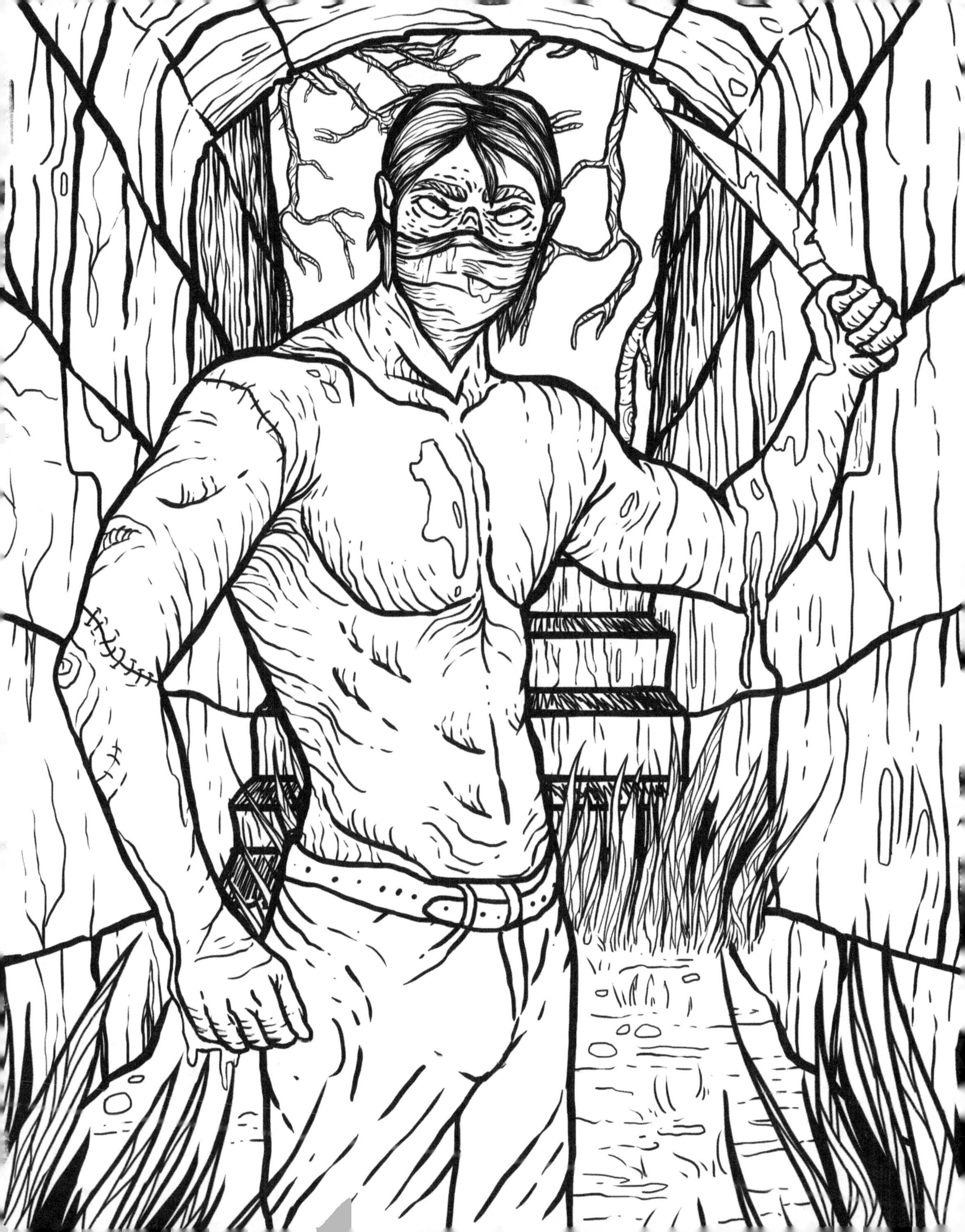

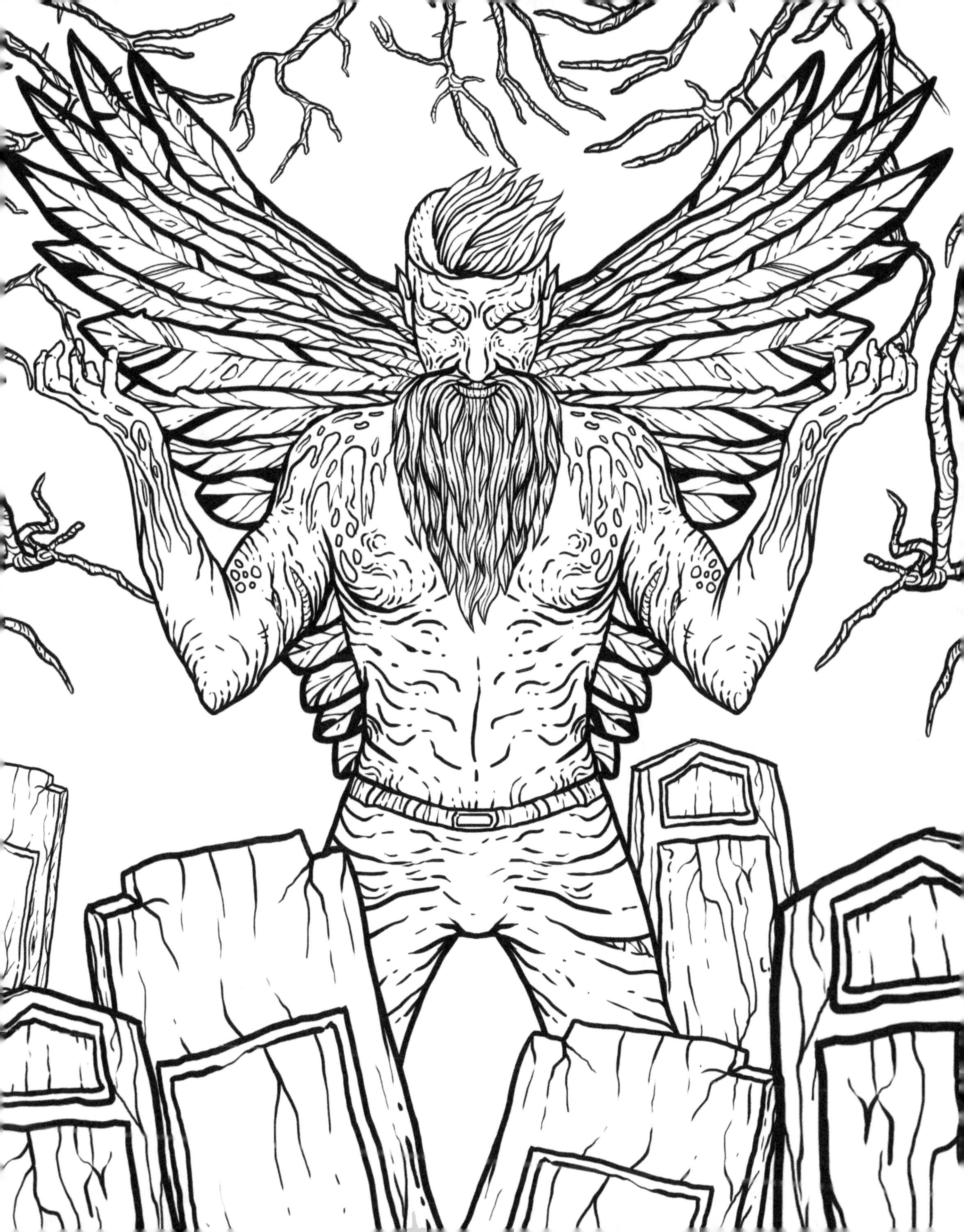

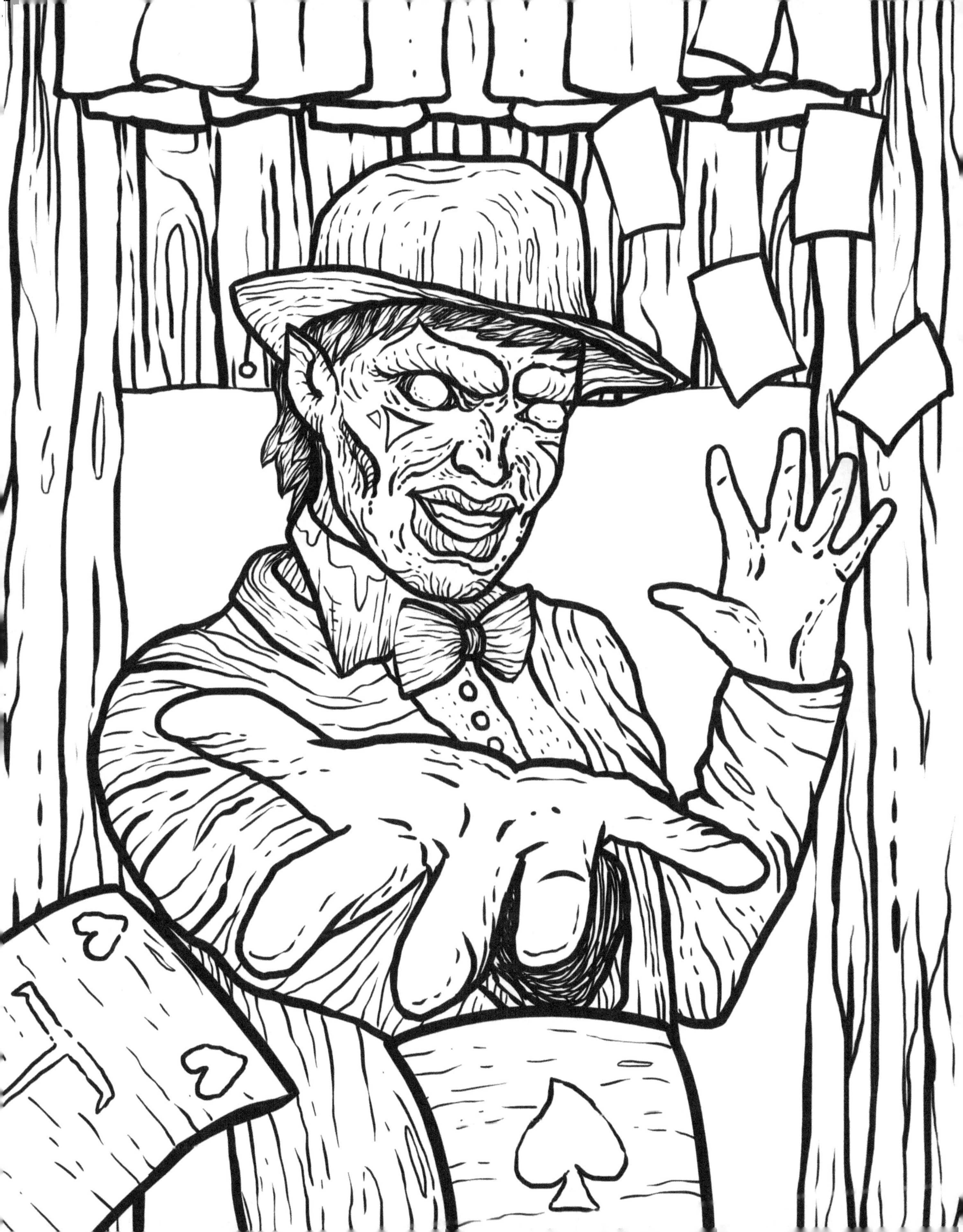

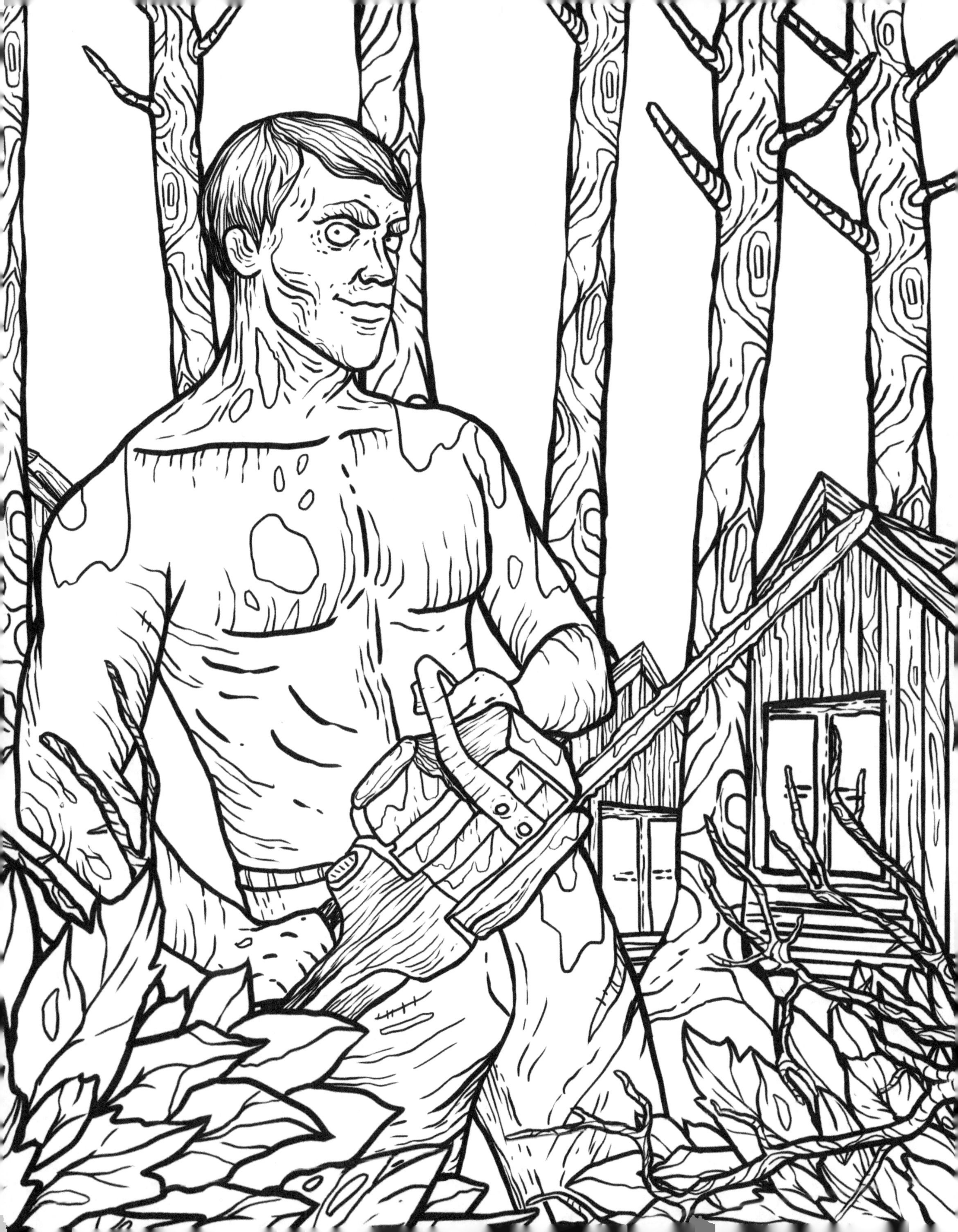

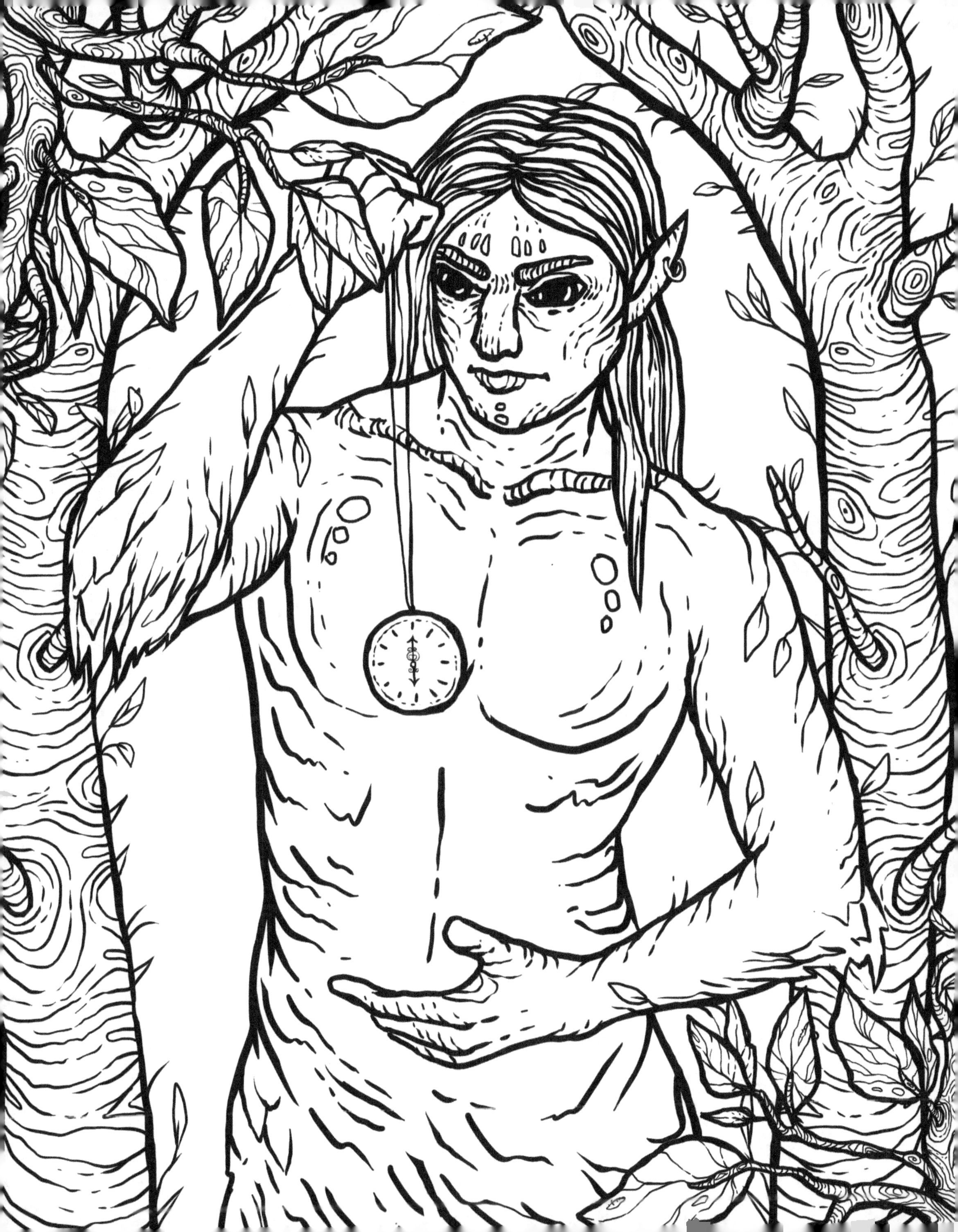

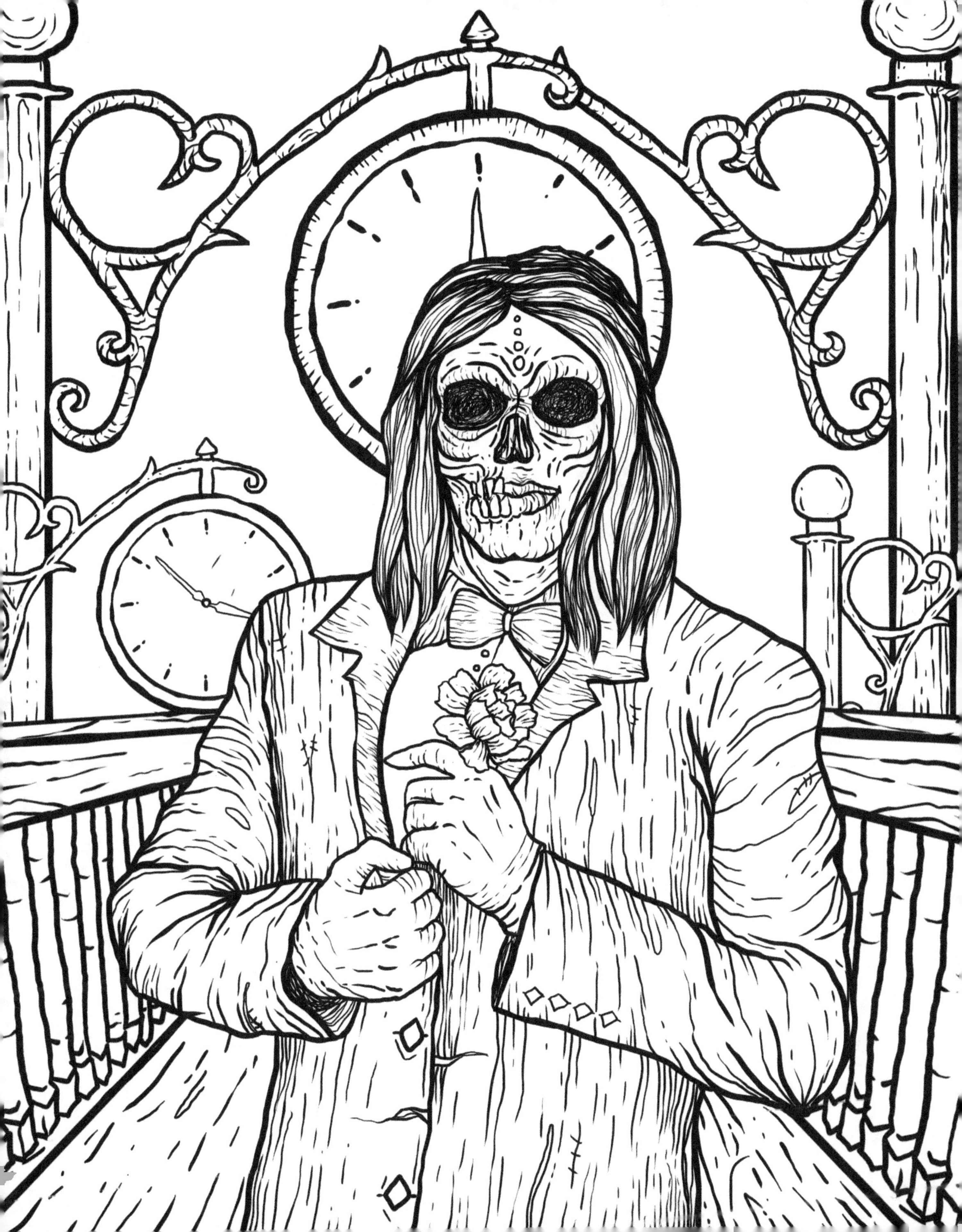

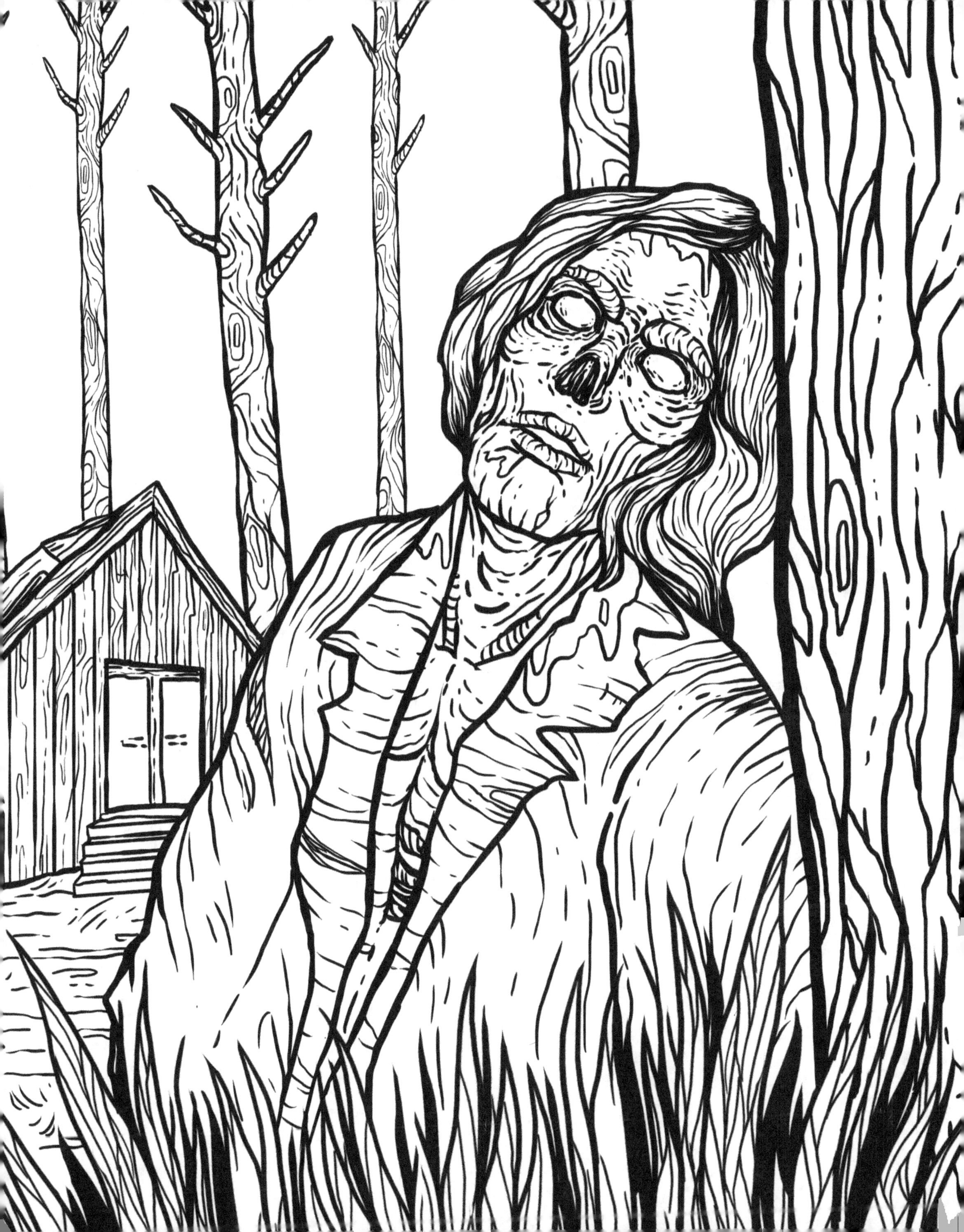

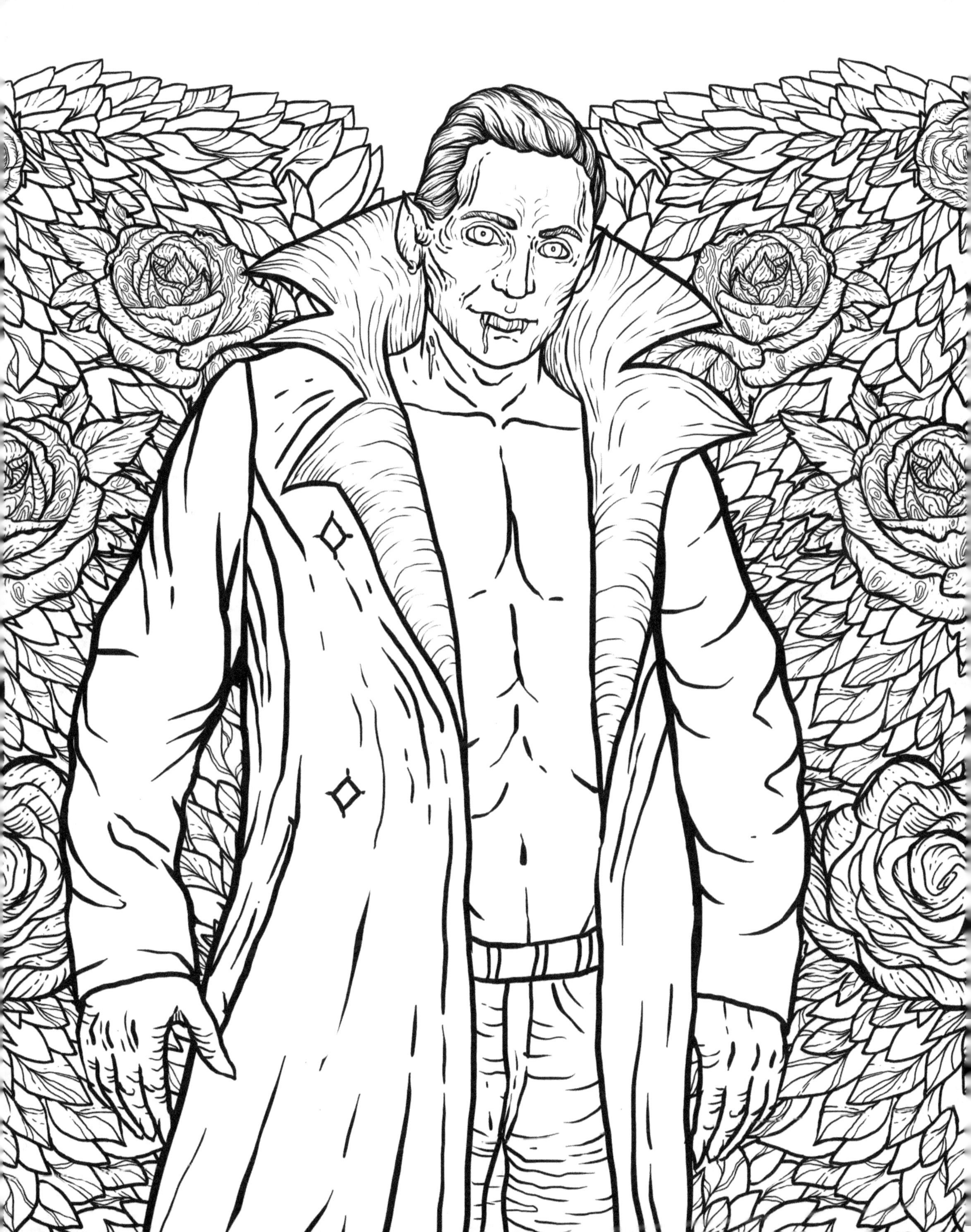

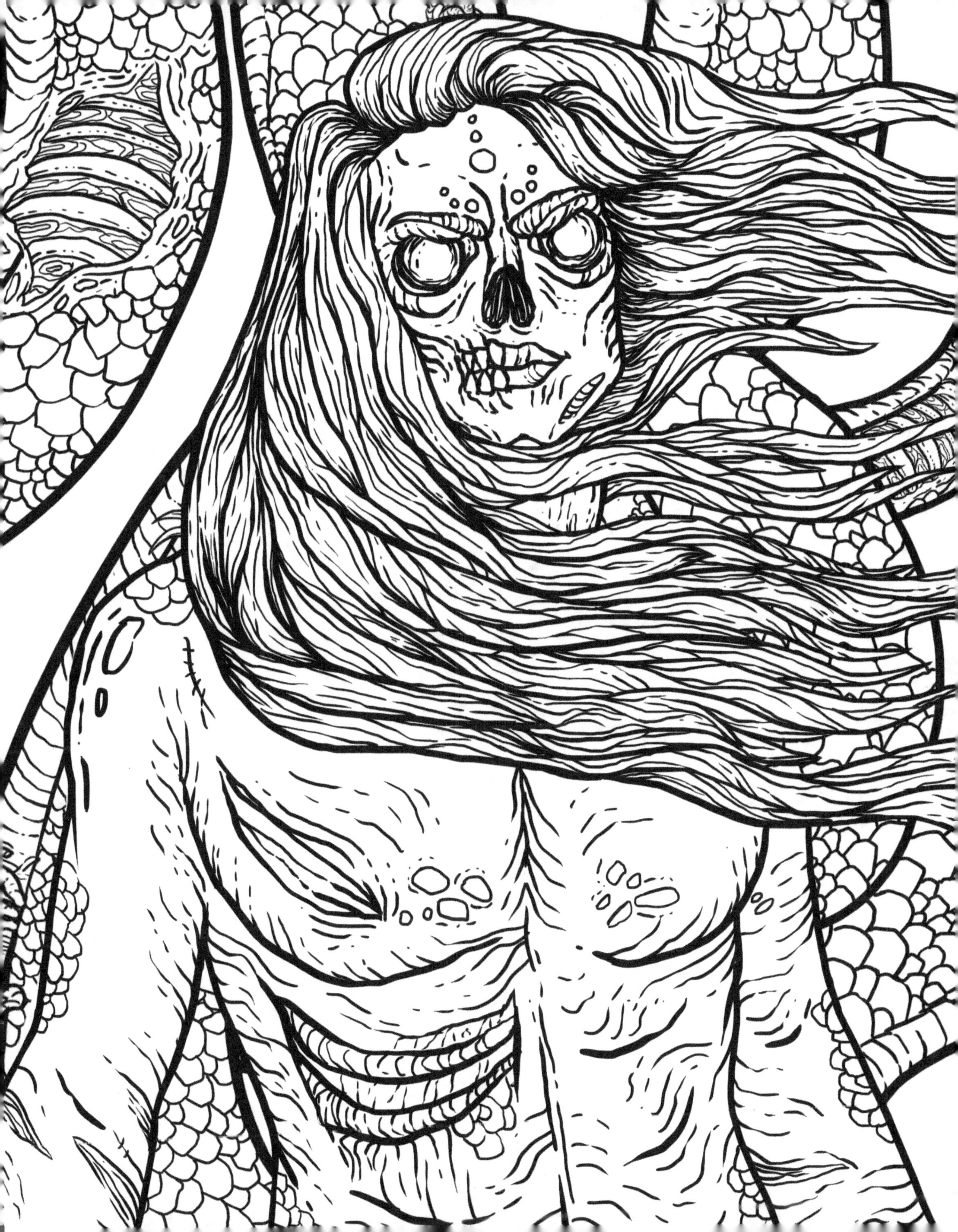

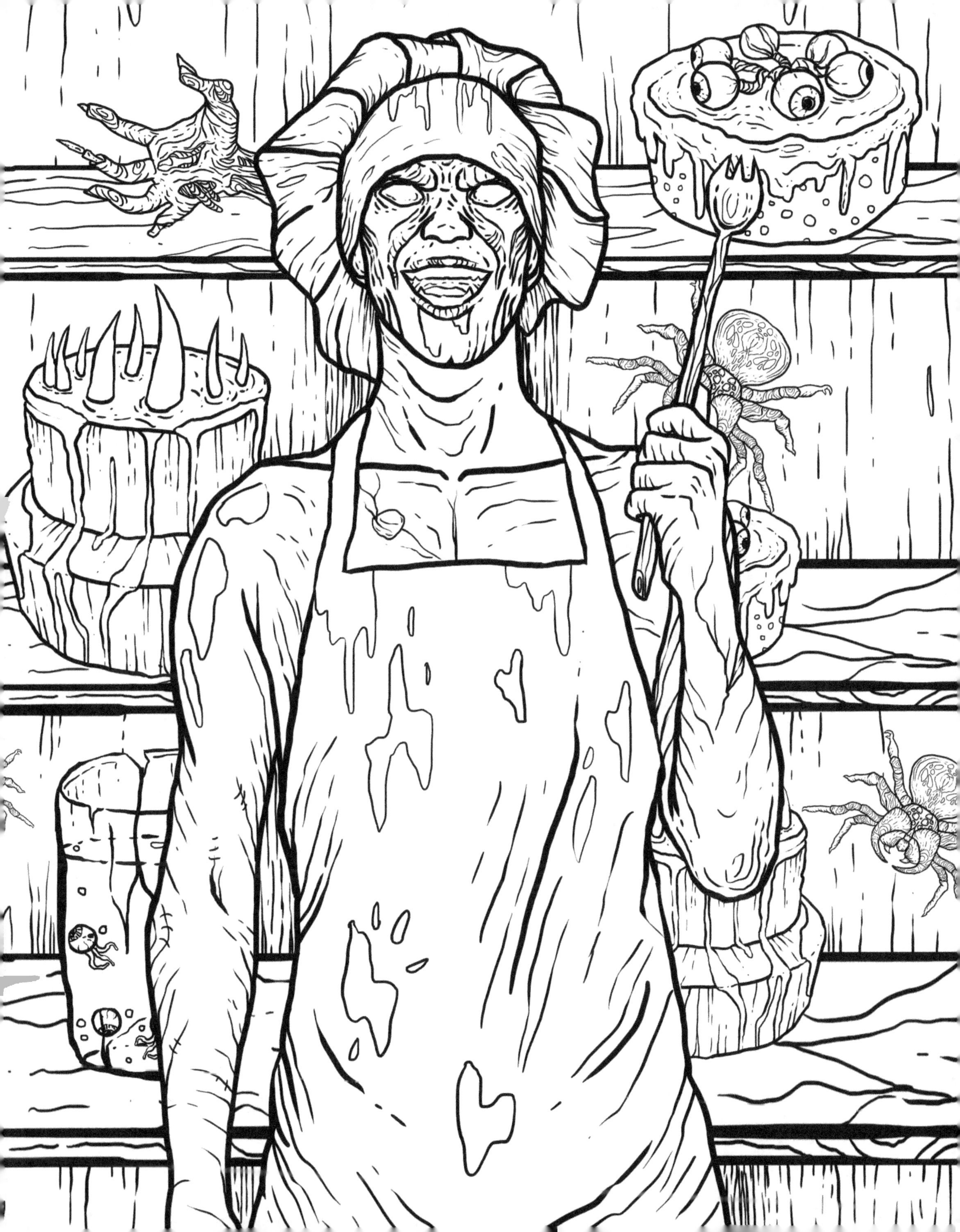

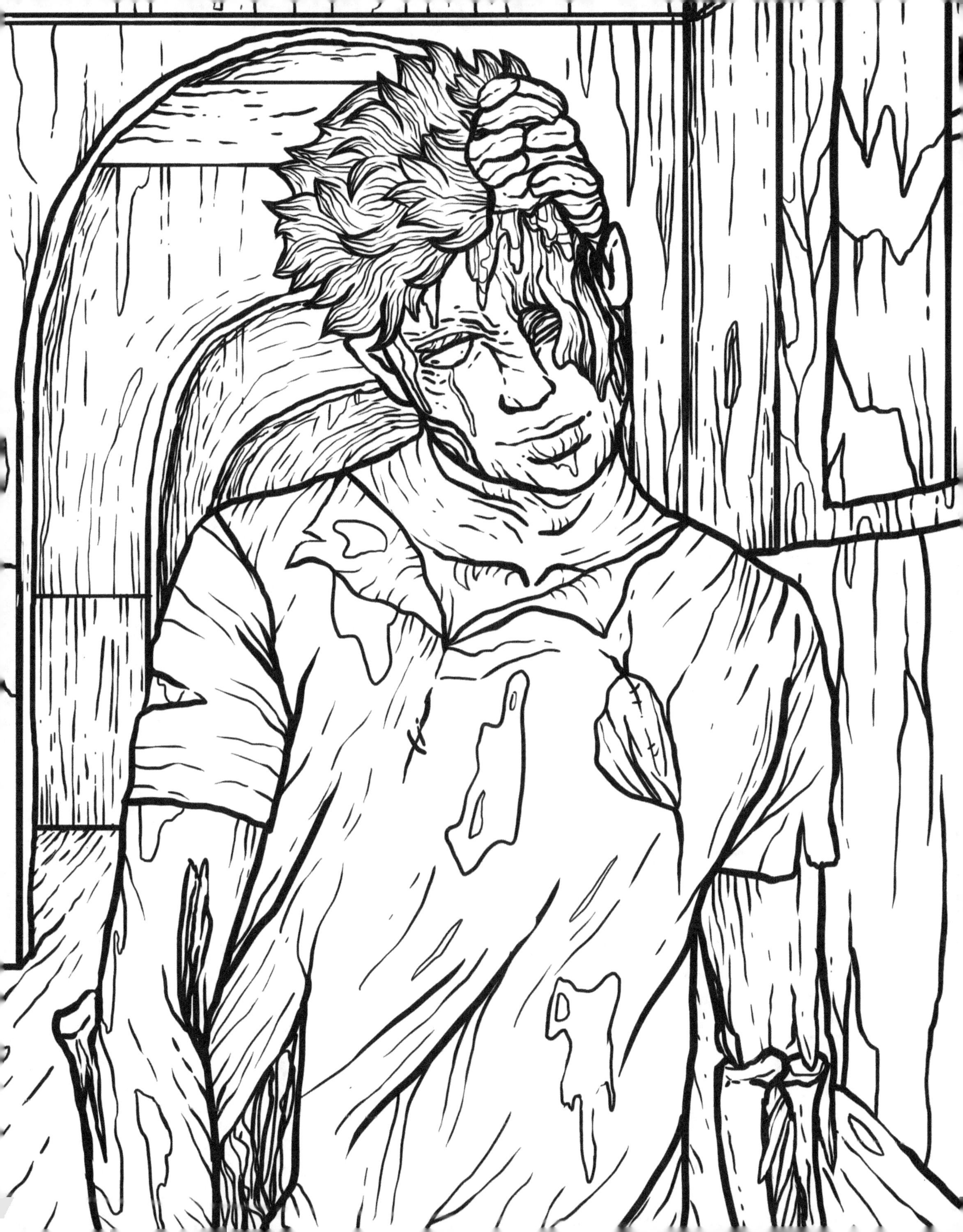

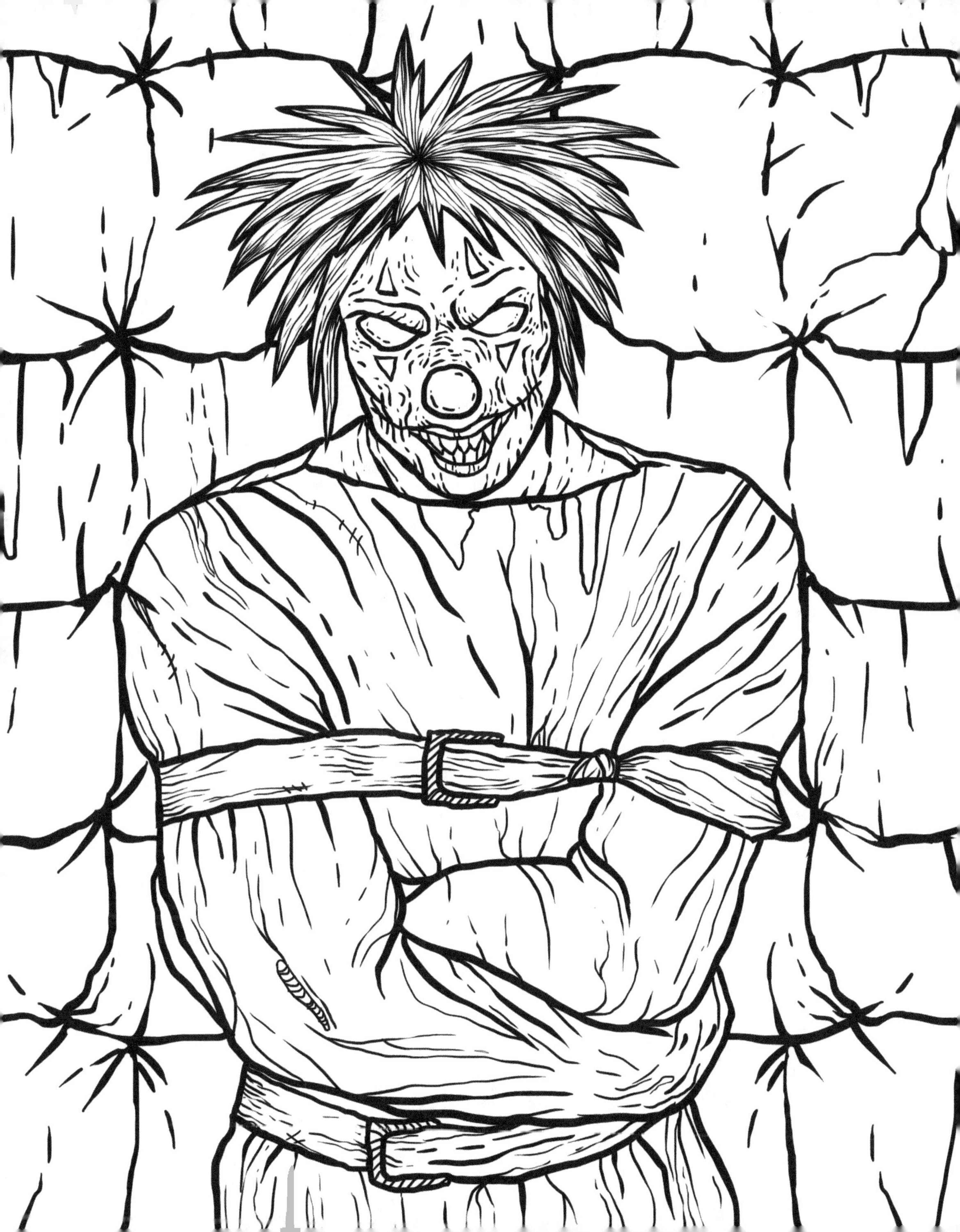

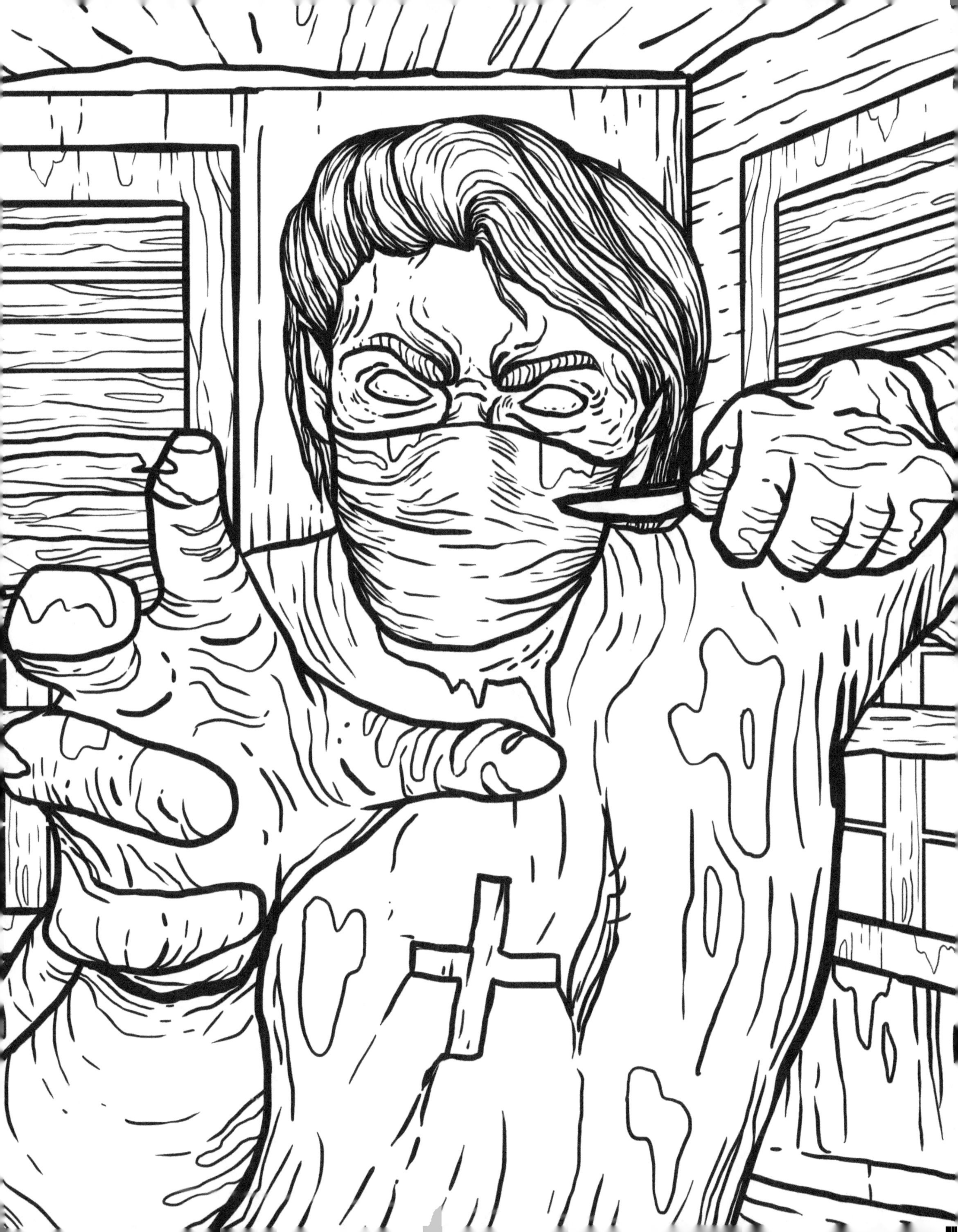

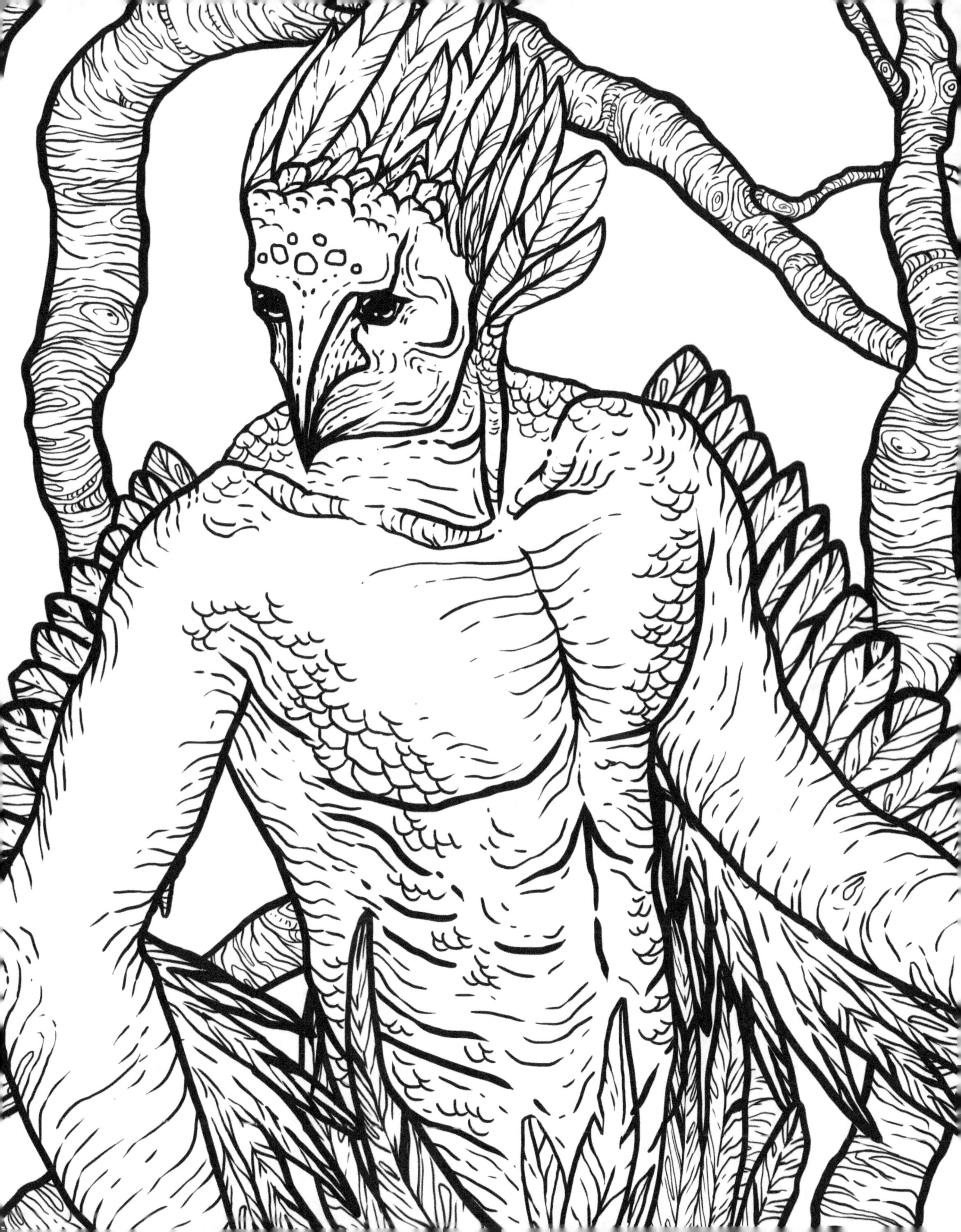

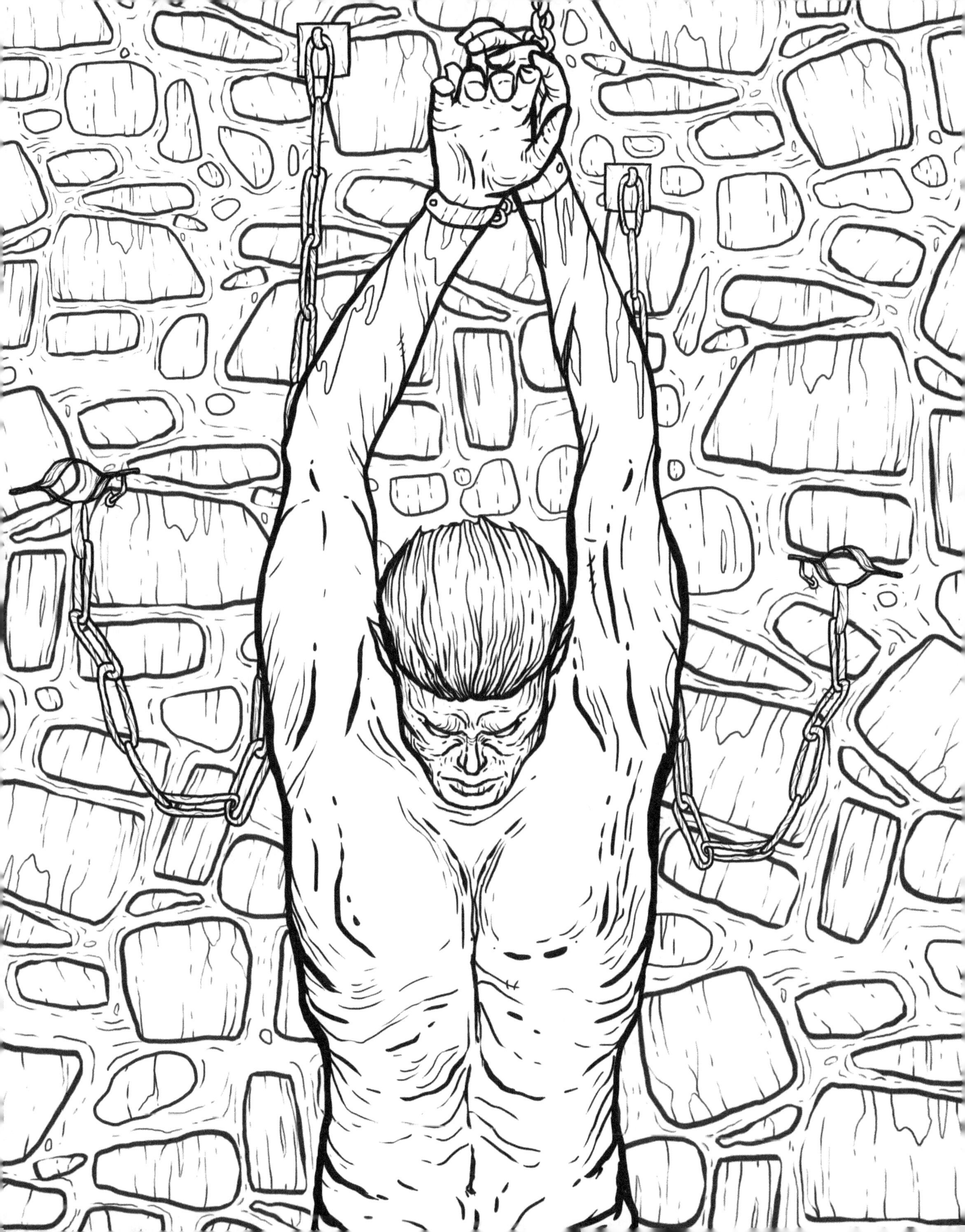

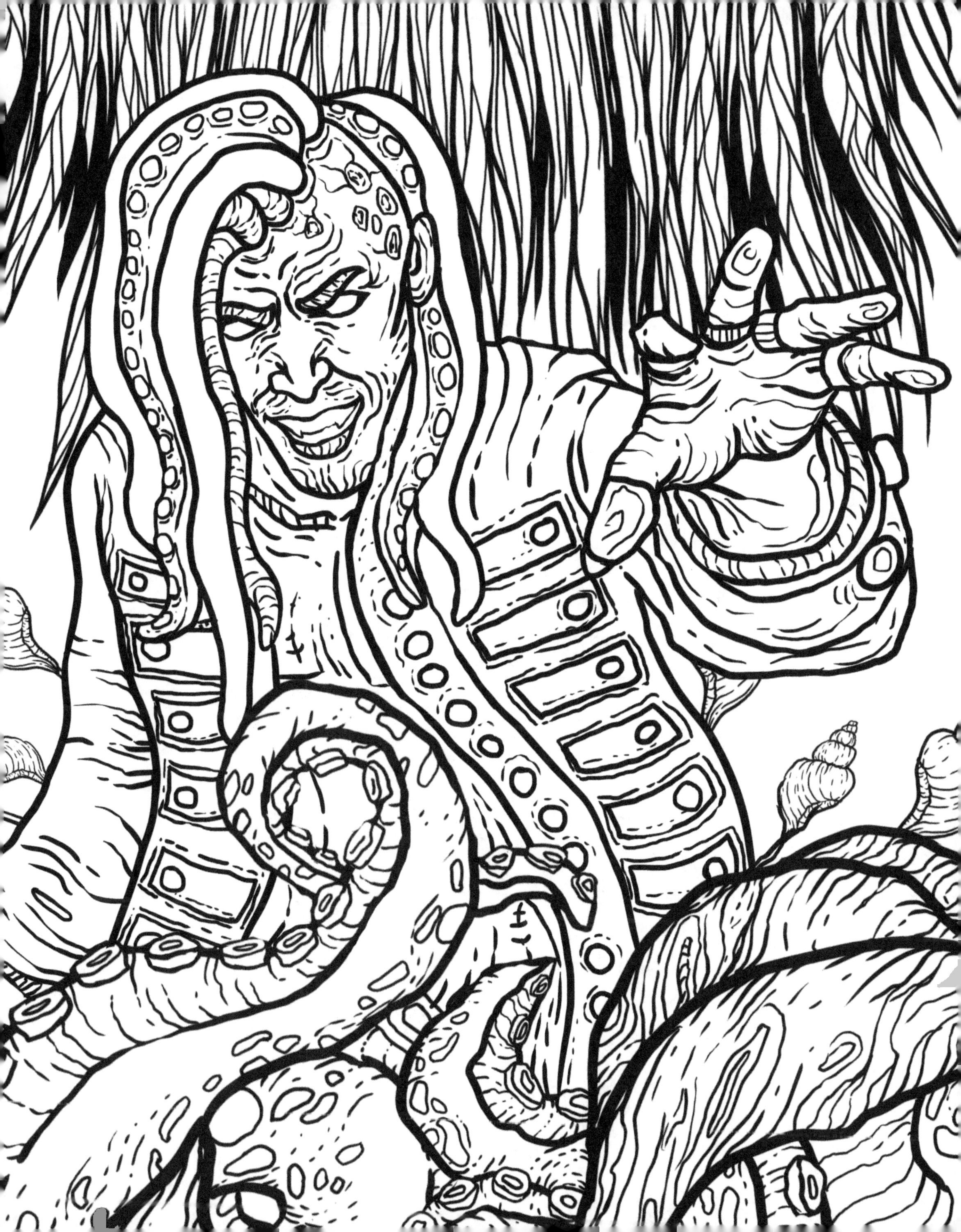

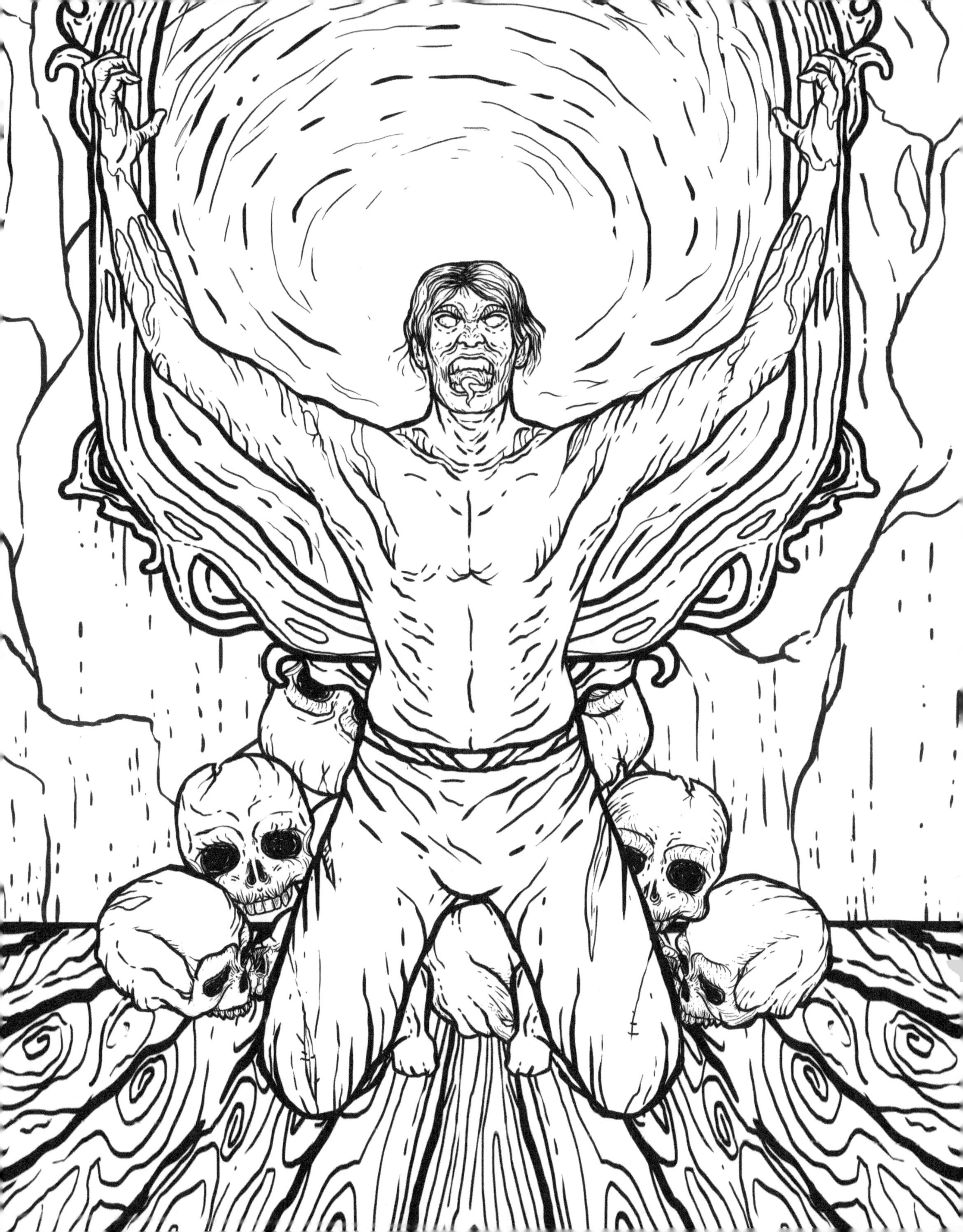

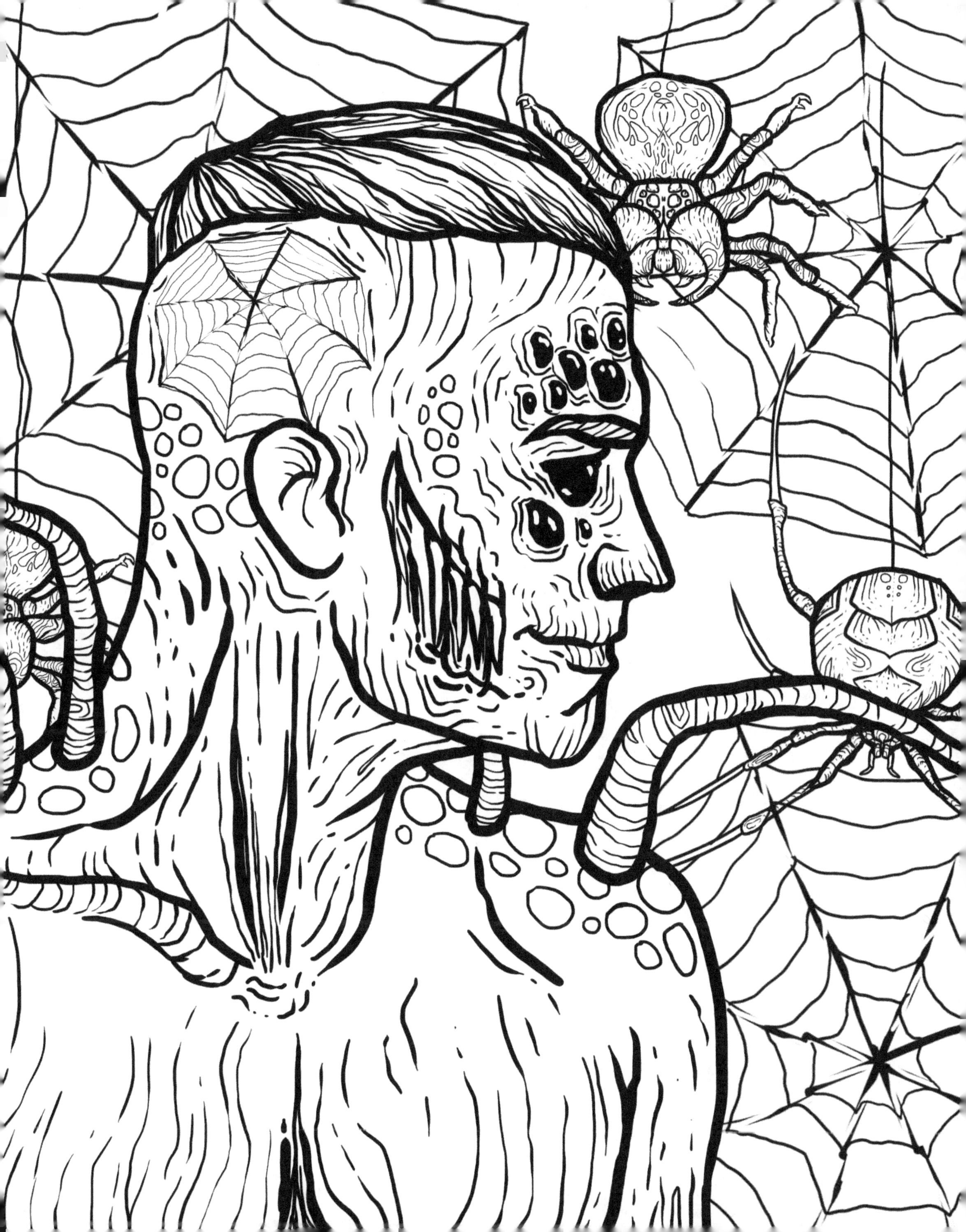

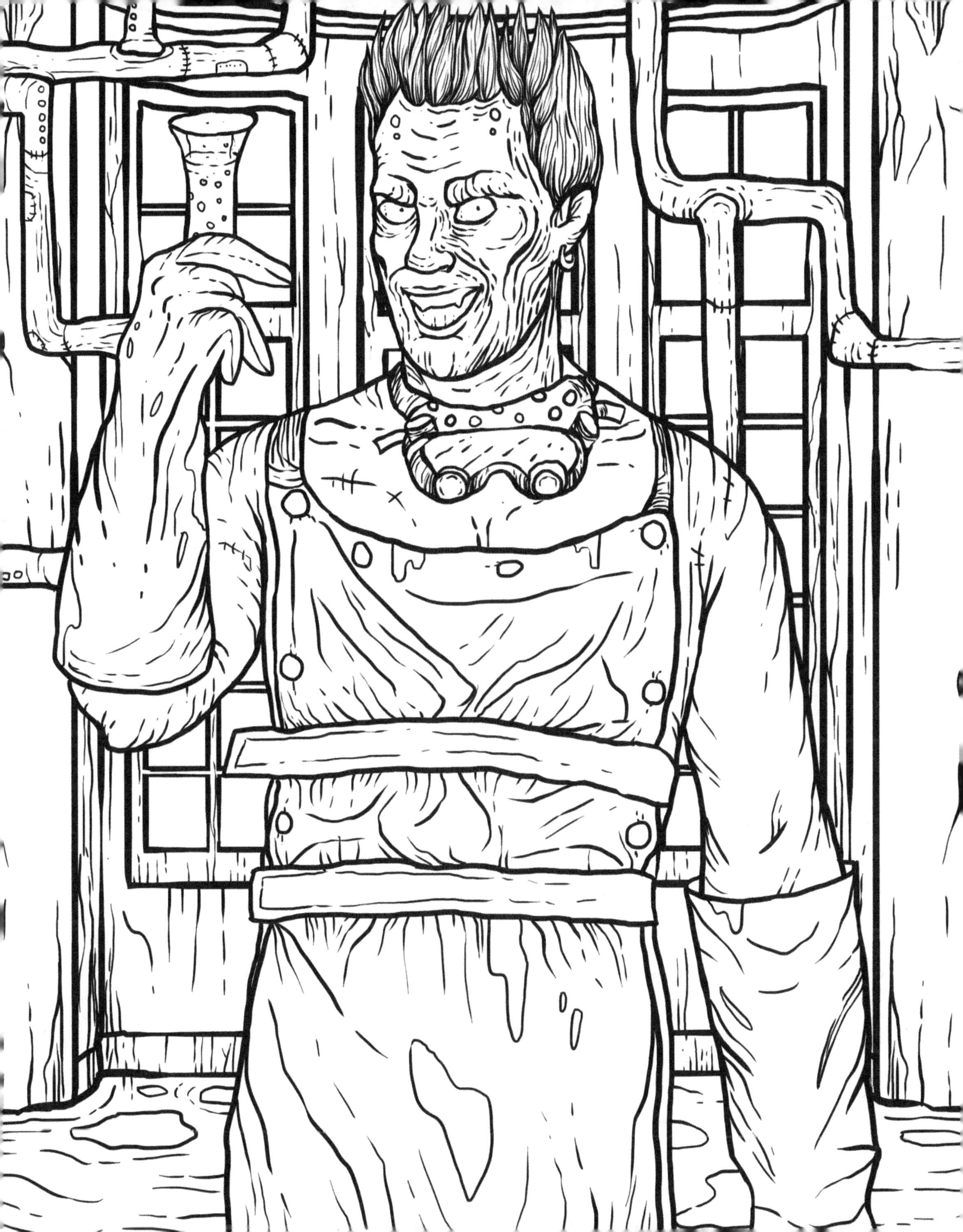

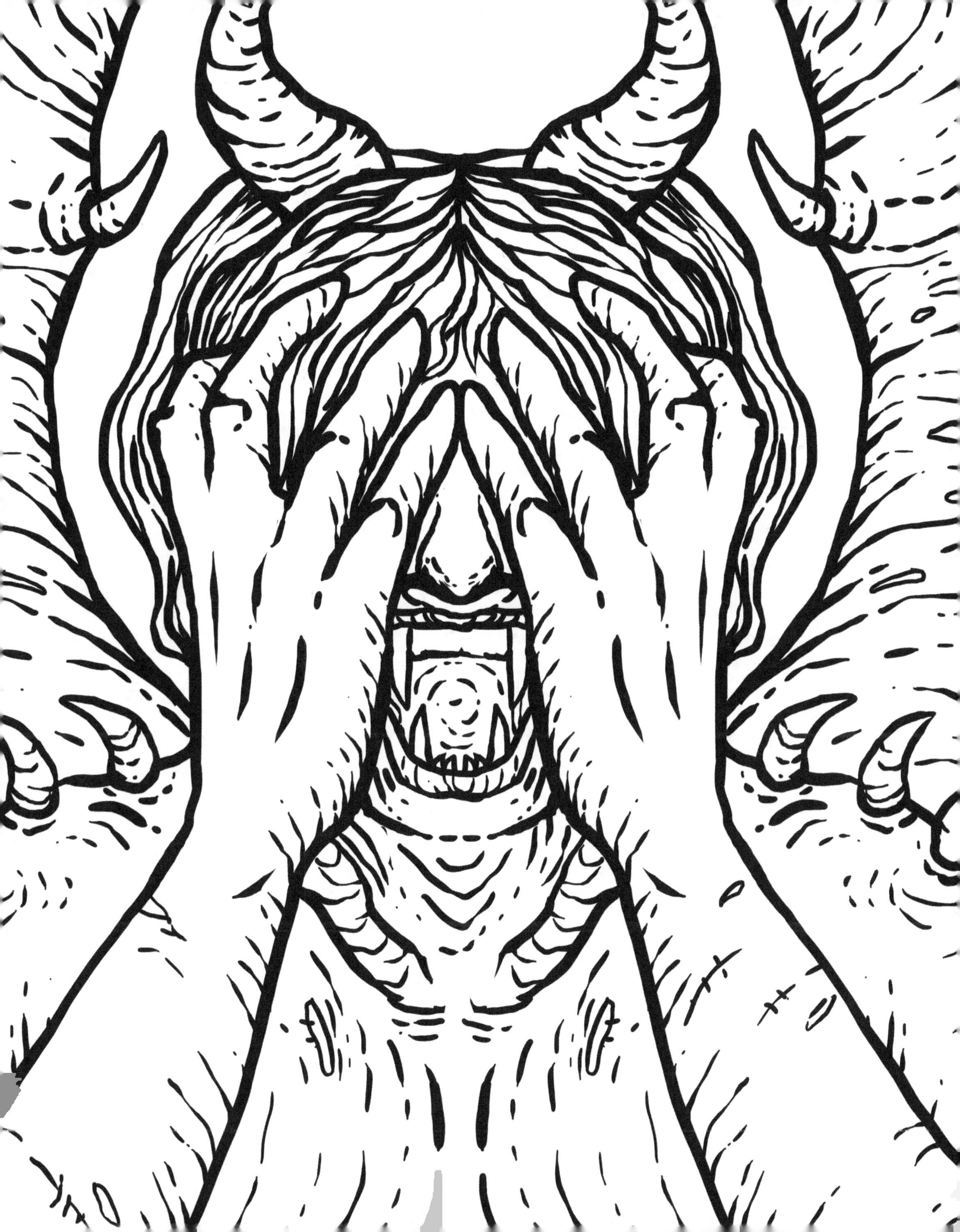

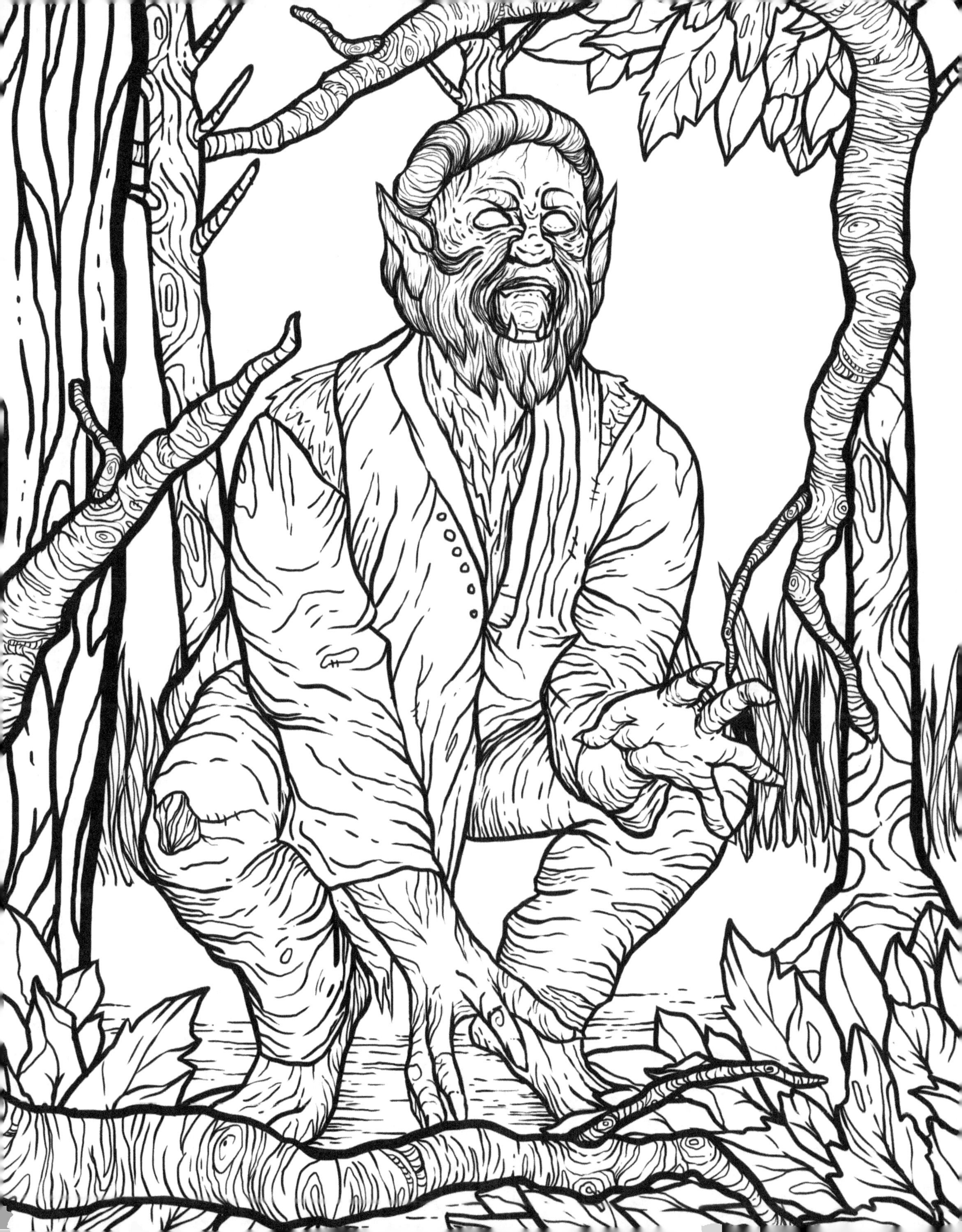

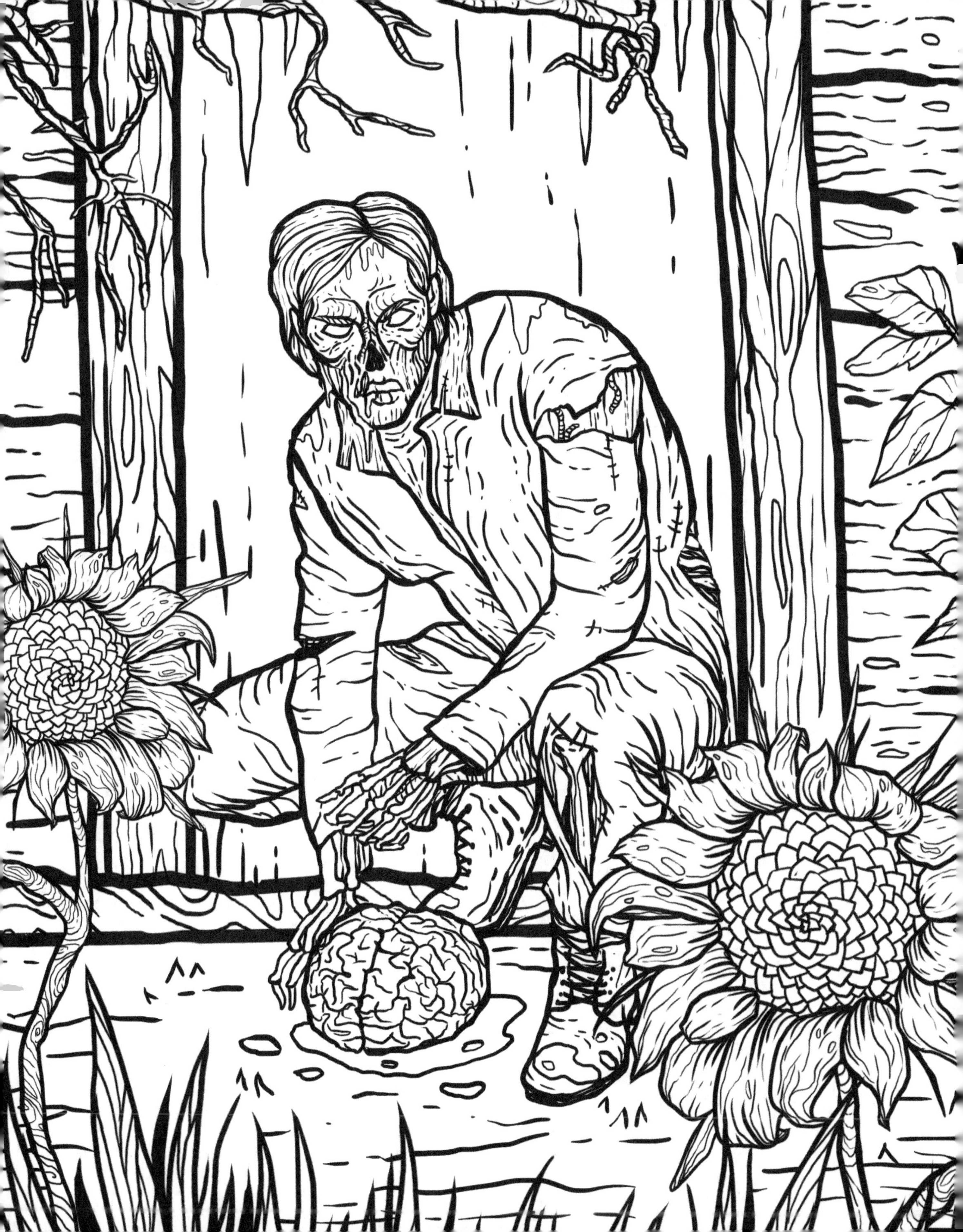